mighty machines
TRUCKS
AND DIGGERS

Written by
Chris Oxlade

Illustrated by
Ross Watton

p

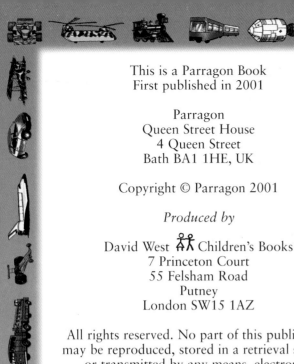

This is a Parragon Book
First published in 2001

Parragon
Queen Street House
4 Queen Street
Bath BA1 1HE, UK

Copyright © Parragon 2001

Produced by

David West ☃ Children's Books
7 Princeton Court
55 Felsham Road
Putney
London SW15 1AZ

British Library Cataloguing-in-Publication Data

A catalogue record for this book is available from
the British Library.

ISBN 0-75254-679-1

Printed in U.A.E

Designer
Aarti Parmar
Illustrators
Ross Watton
(SGA)
Mike Lacey
(SGA)
Cartoonist
Peter Wilks
(SGA)
Editor
James Pickering
Consultant
Steve Parker

CONTENTS

? Which trucks had steam engines?

In the 19th century, the first powered trucks had steam engines, before petrol engines and diesel engines were invented. They looked like the steam tractors used on farms.

Foden steam truck

Amazing! The first ever steam-powered vehicle was destroyed in a crash. The three-wheeled carriage was built by French engineer Nicolas-Joseph Cugnot in 1769, and was supposed to pull artillery guns.

? What did trucks look like before steam engines were invented?

Before steam engines were invented, cargo was moved in wagons pulled by animals such as oxen or horses. This is why the first powered trucks and cars were called 'horseless' carriages.

4

? What was a charabanc?

A charabanc was a flat-bodied truck with benches in the back for passengers to sit on. Factory workers and their families travelled in charabancs on days out to the seaside or to the city. The first charabancs were pulled by teams of horses.

Is it true?
Early buses were pulled by steam tractors.

Yes. A steam tractor was a steam-powered vehicle designed for towing wagons. The first passenger-carrying buses were made up of a wagon with several seats inside, pulled by a steam tractor.

Charabanc

5

Wagon train

Fifth wheel

6

Is it true?
Diesel invented the diesel engine.

Yes. The diesel engine, which is a type of internal combustion engine, was first demonstrated by German engineer Rudolph Diesel in 1897. Most trucks have diesel engines because they are usually more economical and more reliable than petrol engines.

? What is the fifth wheel?

The fifth wheel is the swivelling connecting device on all articulated trucks, behind the cab on the tractor unit. Trailers link on to it. The fifth wheel lets the trailer swivel when the truck turns corners.

? What is a cab-over truck?

A cab-over truck is a truck where the driver's cab is over the top of the engine. The whole cab tips forwards so that a mechanic can reach the engine to repair it.

Cab-over truck

? What gives piggy-back rides?

Truck tractor units are often delivered by being towed by another truck as though they were trailers. It saves money because the trucks being towed don't use up any fuel.

Kenworth piggy-back trucks

? How do truck drivers talk to each other?

Truck drivers talk to each other on citizens' band (CB) radios. They warn each other about traffic jams or bad weather. Drivers use nicknames called handles instead of their real names.

Amazing!
During the winter, some truck drivers build fires under their cabs while they are stopped! When diesel fuel gets very cold it goes thick and gooey, so drivers try to keep it warm and runny so that their engines will start again without any trouble.

Trucker using CB radio

Is it true?
Trucks have up to 16 gears.

Yes. Trucks need lots of gears. They need very low gears for starting off with a heavy load and for slowly climbing steep hills. They also need very high gears for travelling quickly on motorways.

8

Where do truckers sleep?

Some long-distance truck drivers sleep in bunks behind or over their seats. The biggest trucks have a sleeper compartment behind the cab, with a toilet and shower.

Sleeper compartment

Jack-knifed truck

What is a jack-knife?

A jack-knife happens when a truck driver tries to stop, but the trailer slides sideways, out of control. A jack-knife is very dangerous – the trailer might turn over. It is named after a knife with a folding blade.

What is a monster truck?

A monster truck is an ordinary pick-up truck fitted with huge dump-truck wheels, extra-strong suspension and a very powerful engine. Monster truck owners race their trucks over tracks with huge bumps and jumps. The trucks bounce about and even tip over if they go too quickly.

Monster truck

Is it true?
Monster trucks drive over cars.

Yes. In monster truck racing, some of the obstacles that the trucks drive over are old cars! The cars get crushed flat under the trucks' massive wheels.

Bedford Afghan truck

? Who paints trucks for protection?

In countries such as Afghanistan and India, truck drivers paint their trucks with bright colours and religious symbols. They believe that the symbols will stop them from having accidents.

Customised pick-up truck

? What are customised trucks?

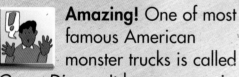
Amazing! One of most famous American monster trucks is called *Grave Digger*. It has an amazing custom paint job, with scenes of graveyards all over its bodywork!

Customised trucks have special parts such as huge wheels, high suspensions and big engines. Some even have boots, bonnets and doors moved by hydraulic rams. Custom trucks are built specially for shows and races.

11

What is a dragster truck?

A dragster truck is customised for high-acceleration drag racing. Dragsters race against each other in pairs from a standing start along a short track. Dragsters have extra-powerful engines and enormous rear tyres to get plenty of grip on the road.

Dragster trucks

Hawaiian Fire Department's jet truck

What is the fastest truck?

The world's fastest truck is the Hawaiian Fire Department's custom built fire truck. This truck was originally built in 1940, and is powered by two jet engines taken from aircraft! It can reach more than 650 kilometres per hour.

Is it true?
You can race trucks.

Yes. There's lots of truck racing around the world. In the USA, drivers race customised pick-up trucks. In Europe, they race big truck tractor units.

? Can trucks do wheelies?

Customised pick-up trucks can do wheelies. They have huge engines and a heavy weight at the rear to help the front rise up.

Leyland truck doing a wheelie

? How do tanks travel?

Tanks are good at driving across rough, muddy ground, but they're quite slow. When tanks need to move quickly, they're carried on special tank transporters. The transporter's trailer needs lots of wheels to spread out the huge weight of the tank.

Oshkosh tank transporter

Amphibious trucks

? Which trucks can swim?

Armies transport equipment in amphibious trucks that can drive on land like a normal truck and float across water like a boat. Amphibious trucks have a waterproof underside to stop water flooding the engine.

Amazing! Some trucks have armour plating on the outside. They're called armoured personnel carriers (APCs for short). They're used to carry troops on battlefields.

14

? What carries missiles?

Missile-carrying trucks transport huge nuclear missiles. On board the truck is a launch pad and a control centre for launching the missile. The trucks carry the missiles into the countryside if their base is threatened by enemy attack.

Russian mobile missile launcher

Is it true?
Some trucks have caterpillar tracks.

Yes. A type of truck called a half-track has wheels at the front and caterpillar tracks at the rear. Armies often transport their troops in half-tracks.

? Which truck scrapes?

A scraper is a truck that scrapes a thin layer of soil from the ground and collects it. Scrapers move and level earth during road building.

Scraper

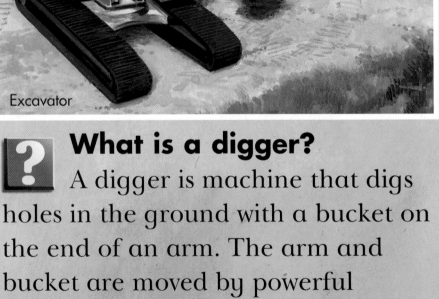

Excavator

? What is a digger?

A digger is machine that digs holes in the ground with a bucket on the end of an arm. The arm and bucket are moved by powerful hydraulic rams. Caterpillar tracks help the digger move across rough, muddy ground. Some diggers are called excavators.

Is it true?
Digger buckets can hold two cars.

Yes. Massive diggers that work in quarries and open-cast mines gouge rock and earth out with huge rotating bucket wheels. Each bucket could hold two cars.

16

Terex Titan

Which is the biggest truck in the world?

The world's biggest truck is a dumper truck called a *Terex Titan*. It's as tall as a house and carries 300 tonnes of rubble. Each of its tyres is twice as high as a person.

Amazing! The *Terex Titan* dumper truck is much too big to drive along public roads. So to get from one work site to another, it has to be taken to bits and carried on transporter trucks.

? Which digger can do different jobs?

A type of digger called a backhoe loader can dig, load and drill. At the back is a digger arm with a bucket called a backhoe. At the front is a shovel for picking up loose soil and rock. Different sized buckets or a pneumatic drill can be attached to the backhoe.

Backhoe loader

Is it true?
Some trucks have bullet-proof glass.

Yes. Demolition machines have extra-strong, bullet-proof glass in their cabs. The glass stops falling masonry crashing into the cab and hurting the driver.

Amazing! There are mini digging machines as well as big ones. Mini machines are used where large machines can't go, such as in basements, and for digging small trenches in pavements and gardens.

Which trucks can reach high up?

A mobile crane is a truck with a crane on its back. Mobiles cranes work on construction sites, lifting heavy objects such as steel girders into place with their telescopic arms. There is a cab at the back for the driver who operates the crane.

Mobile crane

Cement mixer

19

How is concrete delivered?

Concrete is carried to building sites in cement mixers. The ingredients are put in the mixer's drum, which rotates, mixing the concrete.

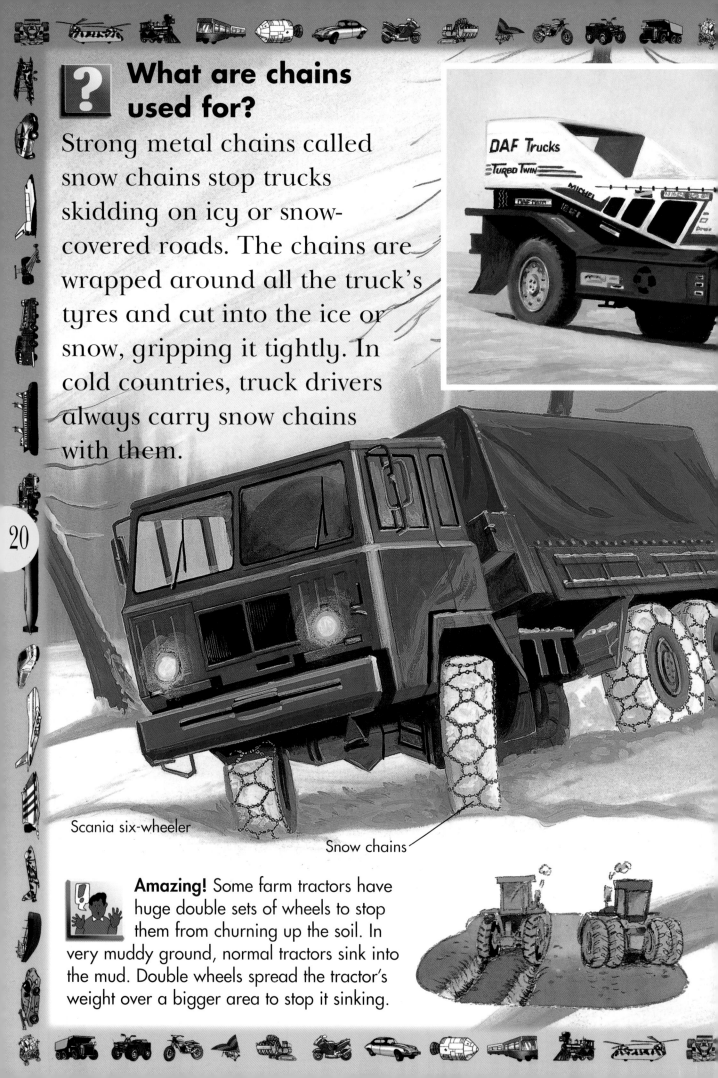

? What are chains used for?

Strong metal chains called snow chains stop trucks skidding on icy or snow-covered roads. The chains are wrapped around all the truck's tyres and cut into the ice or snow, gripping it tightly. In cold countries, truck drivers always carry snow chains with them.

Scania six-wheeler

Snow chains

Amazing! Some farm tractors have huge double sets of wheels to stop them from churning up the soil. In very muddy ground, normal tractors sink into the mud. Double wheels spread the tractor's weight over a bigger area to stop it sinking.

DAF Turbotwin rally truck

Trucks compete in many rallies, including the famous Paris-Dakar Rally that crosses the Sahara Desert in northern Africa. More trucks carry spares and mechanics for other competitors, who race in cars and on motorbikes.

Four-wheel drive pick up truck

? **What is four-wheel drive?**

When a truck has four-wheel drive, it means that the engine makes all the wheels turn. In some trucks, the engine only turns two of the wheels. Four-wheel drive is good for driving off-road on muddy tracks.

21

Can trucks move houses?

Very powerful trucks called tractors are used for pulling very heavy loads. They have monster diesel engines and can drive very slowly. Tractors can even move houses loaded on to wide trailers.

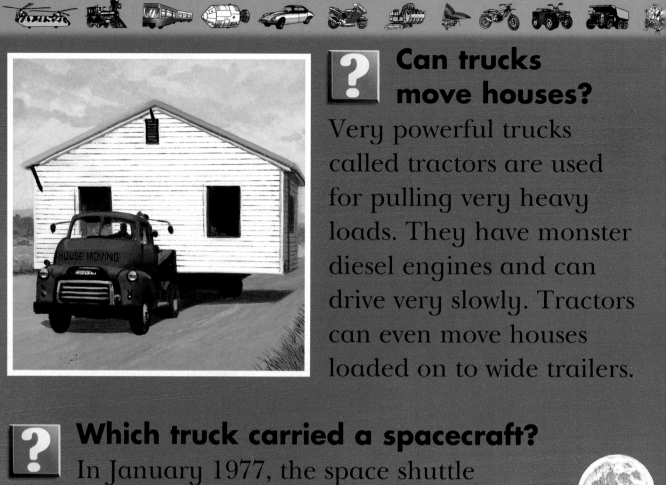

Which truck carried a spacecraft?

In January 1977, the space shuttle *Enterprise* was transported 64 kilometres overland by a Kenworth diesel truck across the Mojave Desert in California. The shuttle weighed 75 tonnes, but the Kenworth was able to pull a load of over 500 tonnes.

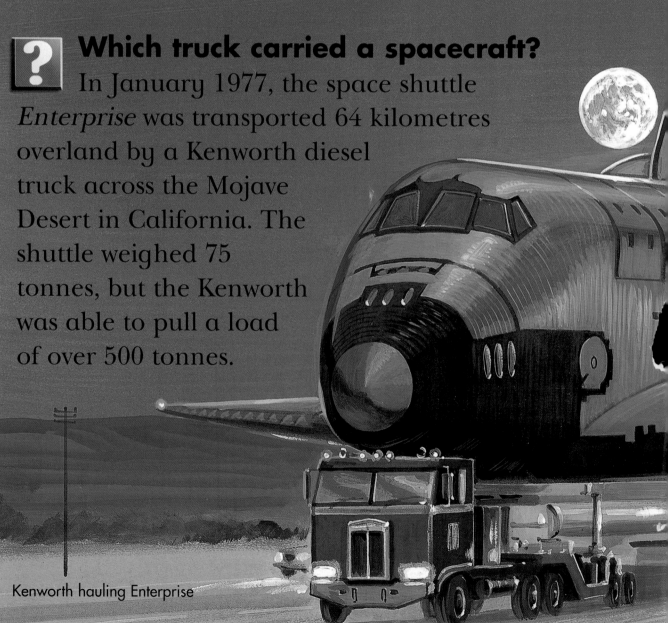

Kenworth hauling Enterprise

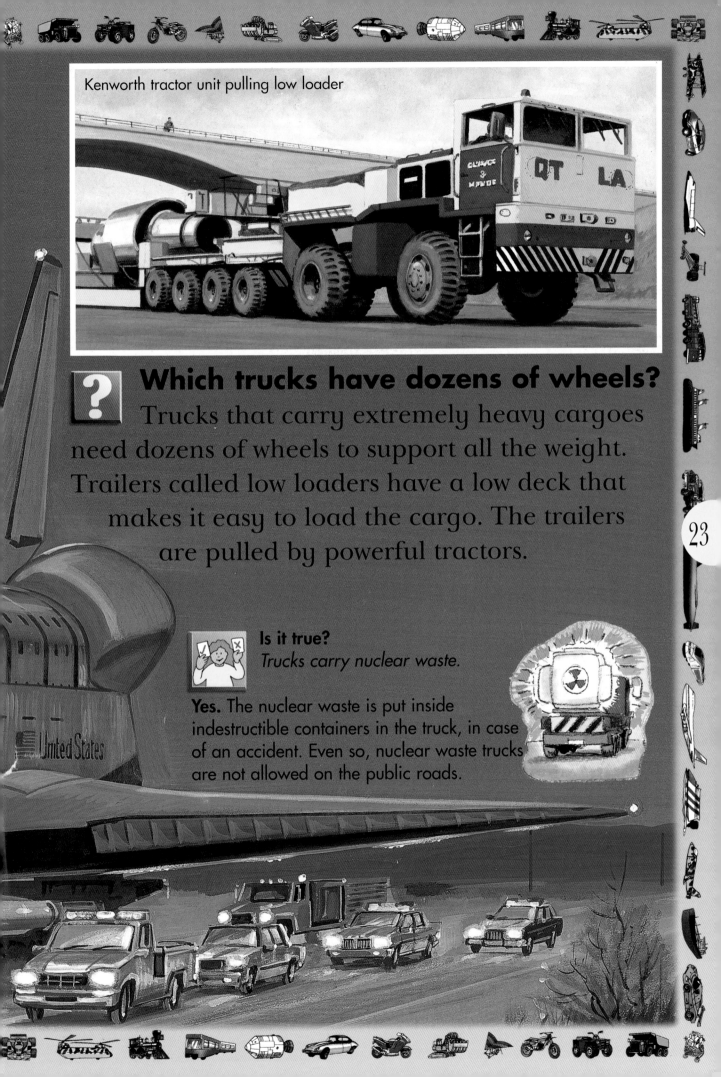

Kenworth tractor unit pulling low loader

? Which trucks have dozens of wheels?

Trucks that carry extremely heavy cargoes
need dozens of wheels to support all the weight.
Trailers called low loaders have a low deck that
makes it easy to load the cargo. The trailers
are pulled by powerful tractors.

Is it true?
Trucks carry nuclear waste.

Yes. The nuclear waste is put inside
indestructible containers in the truck, in case
of an accident. Even so, nuclear waste trucks
are not allowed on the public roads.

? Which fire truck has two drivers?

Some fire trucks carry ladders so long that the ladder needs its own extra-long trailer. A second driver in a rear cab turns the rear wheels of the trailer so that the truck can get round sharp corners to reach fires in narrow streets.

Amazing! Water is pumped along fire hoses by a powerful pump in a fire truck. It comes out of the hose nozzle so quickly that the fire fighter holding the nozzle can be lifted off the ground.

Is it true?
Fire engines need stabilisers.

Yes. Fire engines with long ladders could topple over if the ladder was fully extended to the side. So they have two stabilisers on each side.

Airport fire truck

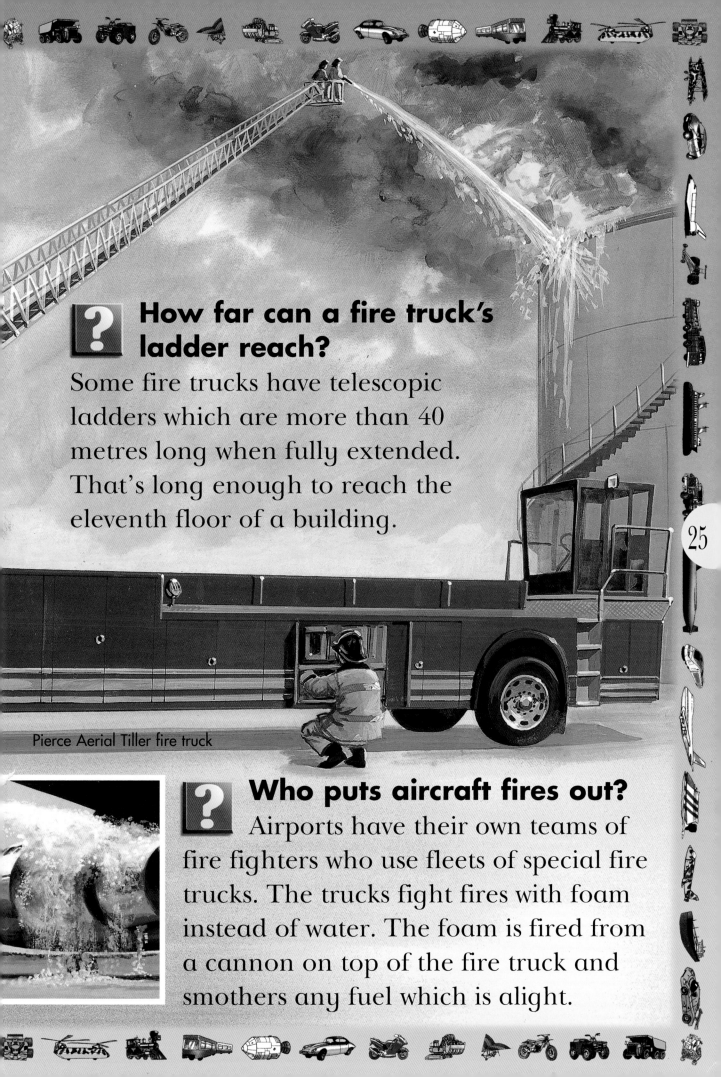

? How far can a fire truck's ladder reach?

Some fire trucks have telescopic ladders which are more than 40 metres long when fully extended. That's long enough to reach the eleventh floor of a building.

Pierce Aerial Tiller fire truck

? Who puts aircraft fires out?

Airports have their own teams of fire fighters who use fleets of special fire trucks. The trucks fight fires with foam instead of water. The foam is fired from a cannon on top of the fire truck and smothers any fuel which is alight.

What is a wrecker?

A wrecker is a recovery truck that tows away cars, buses and other vehicles that are wrecked in accidents, often blocking roads or lying in ditches. Wreckers need powerful diesel engines for towing and a winch for pulling vehicles that have tipped over back on to their wheels.

Amazing! Some cargo trucks carry a mini fork-lift truck with them for loading and unloading cargo. The fork-lift folds up and is carried attached to the back of the main truck.

Wrecker

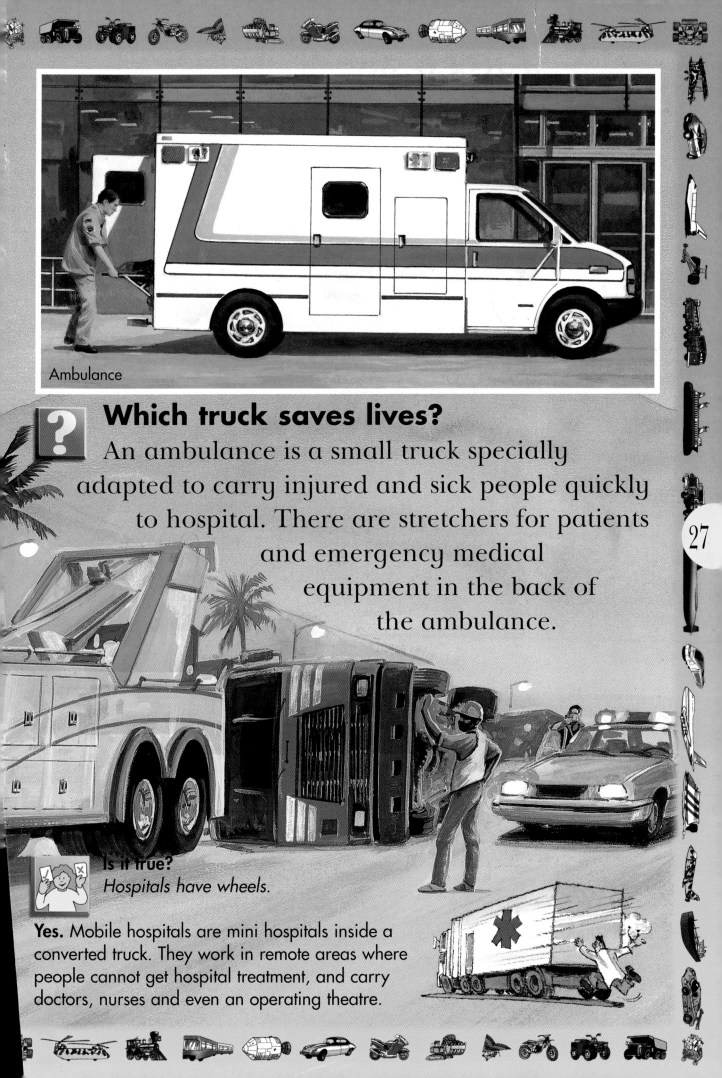

Ambulance

Which truck saves lives?

An ambulance is a small truck specially adapted to carry injured and sick people quickly to hospital. There are stretchers for patients and emergency medical equipment in the back of the ambulance.

Is it true?

Hospitals have wheels.

Yes. Mobile hospitals are mini hospitals inside a converted truck. They work in remote areas where people cannot get hospital treatment, and carry doctors, nurses and even an operating theatre.

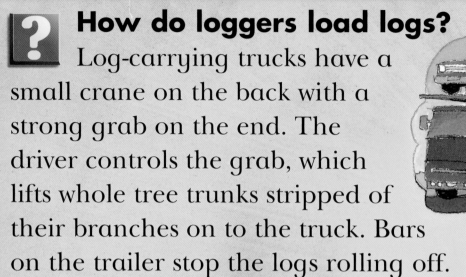

? How do loggers load logs?

Log-carrying trucks have a small crane on the back with a strong grab on the end. The driver controls the grab, which lifts whole tree trunks stripped of their branches on to the truck. Bars on the trailer stop the logs rolling off.

Amazing! Big car transporters can carry up to a dozen cars at once. They have cleverly designed decks and ramps which allow the cars to drive on and off, and fold up so the cars fit into a tiny space.

28

Logger

Is it true? *Tankers carry chocolate.*

No. But tanker trucks can carry almost anything liquid, including milk and oil, and solids such as flour.

? What is a road train?

A truck with two or more trailers is called a road train because it looks like a train travelling on the road. Road trains have powerful tractor units and a big sleeper cab. They are used mainly in Australia.

Straddle truck

What is a straddle truck?

A straddle truck is a type of mobile crane. It rolls over the load it is going to lift, with wheels on each side of the load. Straddle trucks often work in ports, lifting and moving cargo containers.

ROAD TRAIN

Australian road train

? What needs a ramp to unload?

Tipper trucks have a lifting body that tips up to make a load slide out. Sometimes whole trucks are tipped up by a ramp instead! This truck is unloading grain into a grain store.

Grain truck unloading

Garbage truck

Which truck tows aircraft?

Airport tugs pull aircraft around when the aircraft cannot use their engines. The tug has a tow bar that attaches to an aircraft's front wheel. Its low body doesn't bump into the fuselage.

Is it true?
Cherry pickers are used to pick fruit.

No. Cherry picker is the nickname for a truck with a working platform on the end of an extending arm. A worker on the platform can do jobs such as changing bulbs in street lamps.

Airliner tug

31

Which trucks carry rubbish?

Garbage trucks drive around collecting rubbish. A mechanism lifts garbage bins, turns them upside down and shakes them to empty their contents into the truck. Then a powerful ram crushes the rubbish and squeezes it into the truck.

Glossary

Amphibious Capable of moving both on land and in the water.

Articulated A vehicle which is capable of bending in the middle.

Diesel engine A type of internal combustion engine that uses diesel oil as fuel.

Fuselage The main part of a plane where passengers and crew sit and cargo is carried.

Gears Sets of cogs that transfer power from a truck's engine to its wheels. By selecting different sets of cogs with the gear lever, the driver can make the truck start off and travel at different speeds.

Hydraulic Worked by liquid. Liquid pumped to the cylinders moves pistons in or out to make a machine's parts move.

Nuclear waste Dangerous waste material from nuclear power plants.

Pneumatic Worked by air pressure, or containing air.

Steam engine A type of engine in which the pistons are moved inside cylinders by the pressure of steam created in a boiler.

Suspension The series of springs and dampers on the underside of a vehicle. The suspension allows the vehicle to travel comfortably over bumps on the road.

Tractor unit The front section of an articulated truck, where the cab and engine are located.

Trailer The rear section of an articulated truck, where the cargo is carried.

32

Index